Praise for "Befriending Performance Anxiety":

"Xenia Pestova Bennett's approach to this subject is a breath of fresh air. Broadly rooted in calming down our physiological responses, she opens up important areas of exploration with a light touch and keen insight."

STEVEN OSBORNE, CONCERT PIANIST

"Xenia provides simple, step-by-step instruction to help you achieve calm and inner peace. An ideal resource for anyone wanting to quieten the mind, and for performers in any field."

PATRICK MCKEOWN, AUTHOR OF THE OXYGEN ADVANTAGE AND THE BREATHING CURE

"Grounded in her career as a concert pianist, Xenia offers accessible and effective interventions to calm performance anxiety. This book brings together ancient contemplative practices and contemporary science. It's an incredible resource for performers of all kinds and from all walks of life."

KARINA AYN MIRSKY, MA, ERYT
AUTHOR OF *MAKE A DIFFERENCE & MAKE A LIVING TEACHING YOGA: THE SECRET TO TRANSFORMING LIVES WHILE SUPPORTING YOURSELF*
FOUNDER OF YOGA MINDSET COACHING

"LOVE, love, love, this book. Created by a musician-educator this is a veritable gold mine of tools and interventions that have been tried and tested first-hand. Top of the MUST READ list for performers and performance educators, from classical to traditional music - and everything in between."

DR LIZ DOHERTY, *I TEACH TRAD*: PROFESSIONAL DEVELOPMENT FOR IRISH TRADITIONAL MUSIC TEACHERS

"This book is a helpful guide for anyone experiencing anxiety, including performance anxiety. Xenia's instruction is well researched, introducing readers to interventions from different health and wellness modalities and traditions with clarity and approachability. Her explanations on autonomic nervous system regulation through breath work and movement are simple, accessible, and are proven to be effective."

"Empowering wisdom emerges from these pages: the discovery that a slight shift in attention changes your state from anxiety and worry to a widening calm allowing your butterflies to fly in formation."

"The wisdom, kindness and curiosity that Pestova Bennett brings to bear in all her artistic work shines through in these pages, which are full of brilliant approaches to the alchemical problem we all – musicians included – face with turning our demons into something positive and powerful."

"Xenia Pestova Bennett's research exploring the connections between body, mind and musical performance provides a holistic approach to an area that has hitherto been neglected. It is my view that the wellbeing potential of applying Xenia's practical techniques to all areas of life is profound, and I look forward to incorporating them more consistently into my creative practice in the future."

DR ORLA FLANAGAN, PROFESSIONAL CONDUCTOR AND ASSISTANT PROFESSOR OF MUSIC, TRINITY COLLEGE DUBLIN

"Xenia draws many strands together to develop a model of the aetiology of performance anxiety, and how musicians might approach its disruption. I believe it to be a significant contribution to the field."

JAMES BRITTON, OSTEOPATH

"This book is an absolute must if you suffer with performance anxiety. Get it, read it and immediately start accessing a calmer nervous system and more joy in performing!"

RACHEL FIRMAGER, PROFESSIONAL CELLIST, ALEXANDER TECHNIQUE TEACHER

BEFRIENDING PERFORMANCE ANXIETY

PRACTICAL TIPS FOR PERFORMERS
OF ALL LEVELS

Dr. Xenia Pestova Bennett

Brompton Cove Press

Bangor, Northern Ireland

Befriending Performance Anxiety: Practical Tips for Performers of All Levels / Dr. Xenia Pestova Bennett, Brompton Cove Press—1st ed.
ISBN PB: 978-1-7397176-0-5; eBook: 978-1-7397176-1-2

CONTENTS

To the performer inside each of us – may we shine!

CHAPTER ONE

Introduction

Hello! Thank you for choosing this little book of *Befriending Performance Anxiety*. You're obviously already interested in the topic, or you wouldn't be reading this now. Perhaps you can successfully overcome most obstacles in life but feel nervous when it comes to performance nerves. You might be comfortable speaking in public, yet feel unable to play or sing confidently in front of people. Or maybe you just don't like being in the spotlight. While this book is primarily aimed at musicians of all levels of abilities, please read on if you are an educator, engaged in other performing arts, perform in an athletic capacity or are simply terrified of giving a presentation at work, attending an interview or going on that first date.

As a classically trained concert pianist with over two decades of professional stage experience under my belt, I am very familiar with the cocktail of physical sensations, thoughts and feelings associated with performance anxiety. While studying at some of the top performing arts institutions in the world (first at undergraduate, then at postgraduate and doctorate levels), I was surprised to learn that stage fright was not discussed readily. It was implied to be a sign of weakness to admit to being nervous, something everyone wrestled with in private. Nobody knew what to do, not even the teachers, who rarely offered advice. One of the more comical anecdotes from my student days involved a composition professor, who reportedly requested a bucket to be placed next to them by the mixing desk during a premiere performance in case they had to evacuate lunch. Thankfully, the feared expulsion did not take place.

It was not until I was performing professionally and teaching university-level students myself that I started identifying and using helpful resources from a range of disciplines outside of music. I studied complimentary approaches including yoga, meditation, breathwork and qigong, all of which fed into my experience as a performer and allowed me to help more people.

While performance anxiety is finally becoming less of a taboo, there are still few resources readily available to those outside specialist educational institutions. It is my sincerest hope that this little book will address some of these gaps and provide accessible and relevant support for everyone.

The book covers some of the content from my online *Befriending Performance Anxiety* course (https://xeniapestovabennett.com/perform), an in-depth programme lasting six weeks. We will work on the following goals:

- Discovering the science behind anxiety mechanisms
- Learning to maintain focus and deal with mistakes
- Accessing simple and practical tips on what to do before, during and after your performance

I will walk you through a series of clear theoretical concepts and effective practical tasks (inquiries and interventions) that will provide a roadmap for your performance preparation. We will explore the "tool shed" concept of interventions which you can use as and when needed. We will cover functional breathing, cognitive rehearsal strategies and a range of movement and focus routines. You can use these exercises to support your preparation in the weeks, days and even minutes leading up to performance, as well as during and after each performance. We will also incorporate exposure therapy and post-performance support. If you would like to be personally guided through these topics and explore additional areas of performance anxiety support that are not covered in the book, please join our mailing list in the Resources section to find out about upcoming events.

Tend and Befriend

Before we launch into the main content, I would like to share my way of thinking about performance anxiety.

In one of our yoga teacher training sessions, I remember yoga and meditation mentor Sarah Powers introducing an exercise for "befriending difficulty". What an odd concept this was. As a habitual overachiever, I was used to trying to overcome problems by bulldozing through them, "fixing" difficulties or pushing them away. Then it dawned on me: "What we resist, persists". What if instead of pushing and fighting, I stop and look directly at my anxiety and discomfort? Can I hold this experience in my awareness, exploring it with curiosity and self-compassion without judging or reacting? What messages is it sending – are there more holistic ways in which I can support myself overall? This eye-opening realisation planted the seeds for the *Befriending Performance Anxiety* programme.

Another view that incorporates the idea of befriending difficulty is one of the key concepts of Dick Schwartz' Internal Family Systems Therapy (see "Resources"). "Parts work" involves acknowledging and naming the different parts of our system that might be vying for attention or hiding from our conscious awareness because they are too painful to deal with. Befriending them is an important aspect of the healing process (Schwartz and Sweezy, 2020: 135)[1]. Mindfulness guru Tara Brach also teaches pausing and learning to recognise emotions and parts

---

[1] Consider working with a qualified therapist or coach to explore this approach. It can be helpful to supplement inner work with support through yoga, breathwork or meditation: Yoga Mindset Coaching is a process that unites these modalities with IFS (https://www.yogamindsetcoaching.com, 20 January 2022).

we are afraid of without reacting to bring them "above the line" of awareness (Brach, 2019: 9)[2]. If ignored, neglected feelings might manifest in other ways through destructive behaviours or even disease.

"Befriending" nervousness and anxiety does not equate to helplessly giving up, disengaging or stepping back in defeat. On the contrary, it makes us more resilient and flexible through open inquiry and acknowledgement of what is really happening. Fighting against stage fright only leads to further tension and discomfort. Recognising this part of you, learning about how it manifests in body sensations or emotions, asking what you need to feel more at ease – in other words, holding this experience in awareness in a nurturing manner without pushing it away – is the start of a journey to a more balanced and peaceful existence as well as more confident performance.

While I can tell you from experience that anxiety will never go away completely, we can still learn to make friends with it and accept it, which will lessen its intensity. Even though there is no magic fix, we can address the debilitating side-effects of this beastie and find healthy ways to move forward.

So, let's dive in!

---

[2] Tara Brach uses the R. A. I. N. approach to work with uncomfortable feelings through mindful awareness: R = recognise, A = acknowledge, I = investigate, N = nurture.

"Sheddism" is a concept explored by Gordon Thorburn in his little book *Men and Sheds*. The book is about… well, men and their sheds, illustrated with characterful black and white photographs. According to Thorburn, the word "shed" comes from the Anglo-Saxon for "shade", *scaed*, referring to a hermit's retreat. The hermit "assembled things around [them], some with magical significance… strange objects, the importance of which others could not understand" (Thorburn, 2003: 7).

Let us take this concept of sheddism further to include non-physical objects and tools, kept in a *metaphorical* shed. The tools we will work with include establishing routines and interventions consisting of movement, focus, breathing and exposure therapy in safe settings. As with any approaches, these are personal and will vary from individual to individual. You will need to practise them on a regular basis so you know how to access them when needed.

Think of the analogy of an actual garden shed. You have a selection of tools, which are not always required; however, as you never know which one will come in handy when, you keep them all relatively clean and oiled so they don't rust and are ready for action when necessary. You want to familiarise yourself with how they work ahead of time rather than reading the manual at the last minute; this will save you from potential accidents and disasters.

While all the exercises in this book are simple, they are not always "easy": it takes some investment to reap the benefits. I suggest that you try each of them for at least a month, working regularly without overwhelming yourself. That way, they will help introduce a sense of familiarity and normalcy to an otherwise stressful scenario. So do not leave it until the day of a performance to try one of the approaches for the first time!

Inquiry and Intervention Preparation

Establish a "safe space" to practise. Make sure that the surface is level and non-slip, with at least a metre of space at either side, and no sharp or breakable objects around. Switch off unnecessary devices and notifications and make sure that you will not be disturbed.

Anxiety Mechanisms

I would like to take a closer look our new friend, Performance Anxiety. While we know that there is no quick fix, we can learn to work with (rather than against) it. In this chapter, we will revise the functioning of our autonomic nervous system (ANS) and ways to balance and calm it down.

Performance anxiety is a universal experience, a survival mechanism that is hard-wired. The physiological symptoms of anxiety can vary, but many of us have several in common. Participants in my courses are usually reassured to learn that they are not alone and that many others have a similar response. This is a good thing – the fact that we have these sensations means that we care deeply about performing.

We might get a bit shaky (including shaking bow/hands/feet, trembling jaw, wobbly lip); suffer from blurry or narrow vision; have difficulty concentrating; and/or experience physical tension that can lead to reduced technical accuracy, dry mouth, shallow and fast breathing, sweaty hands, cold extremities, gurgling belly, nausea and the need to suddenly go to the toilet. Our blood pressure rises and heartbeat increases, making everything feel as if in slow motion. As a result, we may start to rush, so we must remember to do everything slower than we think we should. These symptoms and more tend to be triggered and exacerbated by new environments, such as performing online or in a different acoustic, on an unfamiliar instrument or with disturbances in the space (for example, audience members coughing or shuffling around).

Even talking about these symptoms can make some of us experience them. This is the sympathetic branch of our ANS kicking into gear. Sometimes described as "fight or flight" (as coined by Harvard physician Walter Cannon in 1915), this is what it says on the tin: we gain superpowers to fight that lion or to flee as blood flow is diverted to major muscles.

While we evolved to go into high-alert mode for short-term emergencies, chronic activation of the stress response without returning to a balanced state is detrimental in the long term. We know that excess stress contributes to inflammation, impedes immunity and increases the risk of disease. In short, you don't want to go into an intense state of high alert every time you perform, and you definitely want to know how to balance your nervous system and return to equilibrium as soon as possible.

So, what can we do to mitigate the sympathetic nervous system (SNS) response? We need to activate our parasympathetic nervous system (PNS), which comes into play once danger has passed and allows for recovery. "Rest and digest" is associated with slower breathing, decreased blood pressure and heart rate, healing, relaxation and the return of diverted blood flow to bring digestive and reproductive functions back online. Termed the "relaxation response" by Herbert Benson in his 1975 book of the same name (see "Resources"), this function is extremely powerful and indispensable for our health.

In his work with patients suffering from hypertension, Benson discovered that we all have the ability to consciously elicit the PNS response and activate substantial physiological changes through calm, concentrated and repetitive activities. These can include meditation and focus/attention training such as silently repeating a mantra or the same word (Benson used the word "one")[3], breathwork, mindful movement and exercise (including tai chi, yoga, qigong, swimming, walking) or other calm and repetitive movement, such as knitting.

---

[3] If you are interested in exploring this style of meditation, the Meditation Trust charity offers affordable training course options: https://www.meditationtrust.com, 11 January 2022.

We will look at different ways to elicit the relaxation response throughout this book as we stock up our tool shed of inquiries and interventions.

Inquiry 1: Becoming Aware

Think of a recent or upcoming performance (real or imaginary). Notice any sensations as they arise: physical and mental. Are you aware of changes to your breathing – is it fast or slow, deep or shallow, rough or smooth? What about feelings, thoughts, emotions? Take a moment to write these down. What are your responses to these stimuli – what kind of relationship do you have with performance anxiety? Is it an enemy, or could it be an ally? Some people like to reframe anxiety as excitement, while others find that SNS arousal gives them remarkable powers (Kabat-Zinn, 2013: 317), sharper focus and enhanced performance (Helding, 2020: 225). What tools do you already have in your metaphorical shed to elicit the relaxation response before, during or after performance?

Breathwork 101

Now we get to the fun part of building our performance anxiety tool shed. The first element we will work with is breathing. As a fundamental part of life, the breath is with us from the moment we are born until the day we die. It moves through the body, linking awareness of the mind with visceral sensations.

You may have heard various claims that breathing can calm your mind, strengthen the immune system and even help achieve higher planes of consciousness. A simple internet search turns up countless techniques and it can be overwhelming to know where to start. There is also a lot of conflicting advice, some of which is scientifically unfounded or even dangerous for people with certain health conditions. It is important to go slow, remain mindful and listen to your body, so please do so as you try the exercises below. Working individually with a qualified instructor can be invaluable to ensure that you correct any unhealthy underlying breathing patterns – see "Resources" for a directory of qualified breathing instructors by area.

In this chapter, we will learn about healthy breathing patterns and how breathing techniques can manage stress and anxiety. These are just some of the approaches you can try: there are many other wonderful and helpful methods and instructors out there, so take what resonates with you. As we continue building our tool shed in subsequent chapters, we will add and elaborate on simple breathing exercises to activate the relaxation response. We will draw on the ancient and established practices of yoga pranayama (*prana* = breath or life force energy, *pranayama* = restraint or control of energy) and supplement our learning with the latest scientific research of the Oxygen Advantage® method[4].

Breathing is intimately connected with stress levels. The breath becomes fast and shallow when we are excited and slows down when we feel calm. Psychological experiences of anxiety can exacerbate the physiological symptoms, and vice versa. You may have guessed this means that we can also influence our ANS by consciously slowing and calming our breathing – and you're right! We can use breathing to send messages to the brain and influence changes in

---

[4] https://oxygenadvantage.com, 11 January 2022. This method is based on the work of Russian physician Konstantin Pavlovich Buteyko (1923 – 2003), https://buteykoclinic.com/about-dr-buteyko/, 12 January 2022.

mental and emotional states through the respiratory
system.

However, beware of the common advice to "take a
deep breath" when you feel anxious. This is not
necessarily a good idea. Why? Depending on
underlying breathing patterns, some people take
"deep" breathing to mean "big" breathing, which
can lead to hyperventilation and activate the fight-
or-flight response (McKeown, 2021: 13). Some of us
might also tend to breathe into the upper chest, using
auxiliary muscles reserved for emergency function, or
take a big breath in through the mouth. Both upper
chest and mouth breathing are directly connected
with the SNS, so gulping a few huge breaths before a
challenging situation can in fact make you feel more
nervous instead of calming you down.

Chronic Hyperventilation

While there isn't a "wrong" way and you certainly
already know how to breathe, there are more and less
optimal ways to do so (Cornett, 2019: 96). One of the
most common breathing pattern disorders is chronic
hyperventilation, or breathing too much. Chronic
hyperventilation doesn't mean visibly gasping for air
or going into a panic attack. It can be subtle and
gradually build into a habit. Anxiety and breathing
through the mouth when talking can lead to mild
hyperventilation, which adds up over time. Habitually
yawning or sighing can be signs of this pattern.
Chronic hyperventilators include people with asthma,
allergies, anxiety, heart disease and sleep apnoea as

well as those who use their voice to make a living, such as teachers or salespeople (Rothenberg, 2020: 97). I suspect that many musicians fit into this category as well.

So, why is even subtle hyperventilation a problem? When we over-breathe, we blow off too much carbon dioxide (CO_2). We might think of this as a waste gas, but it is only in the presence of CO_2 that oxygen is released into the tissues and organs from haemoglobin (a protein in the blood). CO_2 also acts as a dilator for blood vessels and airways, increasing circulation, easing breathing and helping the body relax.

Our body has clever in-built "sensors" or chemoreceptors to continuously monitor CO_2 levels. If we go through a period of elevated breathing, such as during a time of stress, the body can eventually adjust to the new "norm" and reset this sensitivity to a lower setting. Even if we try to breathe less once the stress subsides, it might feel like we are short of breath due to the new habit. The good news is that it is possible to gradually recalibrate to normal through a series of graded exercises, some of which we will try together[5].

---

[5] If you would like to explore more, my online courses on breathing offer in-depth instruction and guidance: https://xeniapestovabennett.com/wellbeing/breath, 11 January 2022.

Humans evolved to breathe through the nose to filter, humidify and warm the air. This means breathing in *and out* through the nose, most of the time (including at rest, when sleeping and during exercise – unless sprinting, doing an intense workout or playing certain musical instruments!). As we learned above, mouth breathing is associated with fight-or-flight and is an emergency response, so should be avoided when at rest. This might feel strange to many of us at first, especially if we suffer from stuffed nose, allergies, asthma or related conditions. However, as we learn to breathe through our nose, stuffy and closed airways will start opening up more – a delightful paradox that makes the effort worthwhile.

Diaphragmatic Breathing

Breathing through the nose also encourages diaphragmatic breathing, which is a natural and calming functional breathing pattern. As opposed to the mouth/upper chest SNS combination, diaphragmatic breathing is directly linked with the PNS relaxation response. You might also know this as "belly breathing". We don't have lungs in our bellies of course, but the belly moves out of the way when we breathe in, allowing the lungs to expand. The diaphragm, a dome-shaped muscle that separates the chest from the abdomen, needs to extend downwards to allow the lungs to inflate, while the belly gently moves outwards with every inhale to accommodate this, coming back with the exhale and massaging abdominal organs. Yoga educator Leslie Kaminoff compares this concept to an accordion, which is the thoracic cavity, sitting on top of a water balloon, the abdominal cavity (Kaminoff, 2012: 5).[6] At the same time, our whole shape is fluid and the ribs also move with every breath.[7]

In some instances, prolonged anxiety or unhealthy cultural body image expectations can lead people to hold the belly tight and breathe more into the upper chest. This type of breathing leads to chronic tension in the back, shoulders and neck as well as further anxiety and hyperventilation (Farhi, 1996: 79-80). It might take a while to start releasing ingrained patterns of tension, but it is possible – we just have to be gentle and take the time we need.

Healthy breathing that uses the diaphragm also leads to functional movement by encouraging good posture through core stability, spine stability and balance (McKeown, 2021: 156). This in turn helps prevent fatigue and injury – another excellent reason for everyone to address underlying breathing patterns.

---

[6] An illustrated video is available at https://youtu.be/KXWG0qxgSyA, 12 January 2022.

[7] It is also worth noting that abdominal muscles are secondary for breathing - our primary breathing muscles are the diaphragm and the intercostal ribcage muscles (O'Connor, 2021: 197).

Take note as you go through your day: are you breathing in and out through the nose when you go for a walk, clean up after dinner, watch your favourite shows, type emails, make love, take a shower? What about during mild-to-moderate physical exercise? Work on gradually training yourself to breathe through the nose during these times. Are you aware of mouth breathing at night? If you snore, have sleep apnoea or wake up feeling exhausted and with a dry mouth, the answer is likely yes. Weird as this might sound, taping the mouth with special gentle tape will encourage nasal breathing and help open airways as you sleep. Even if you suffer from a stuffy nose, it will never close up fully when the mouth is taped. This is a safe method and is surprisingly easy to get used to – you won't suffocate. You can use hypoallergenic micropore paper tape, or the specially designed option that is applied around the mouth to encourage the muscles to engage: https://myotape.com (11 January 2022)[8].

Inquiry 3: Belly or Chest?

Are you allowing the belly to soften and gently expand outwards when you breathe in? Take a moment to

---

[8] Please consult your doctor first if you have pre-existing medical conditions that might be affected and consider working with a qualified Oxygen Advantage® or Buteyko Method instructor – see "Resources" at the end of the book.

check. You can do this exercise either sitting comfortably upright or lying on your back with the knees bent and soles of the feet on the floor to release the lower back. Place one hand on your chest and the other on your belly: illustrations of these positions are available at https://xeniapestovabennett.com/breathing-positions/ (12 January 2022). Observe the natural movement of the breath. Which hand moves more – the one on the chest, or the one on the belly? If the hand on the belly is relatively still, is it possible to encourage the belly to release so that the hand moves? If lying down, you can also experiment by placing an object such as a box of tissues or a soft toy, encouraging it to rise and fall[9]. There is no need to take in loads of air: think of it as gently slowing and filtering the flow. Notice how you feel and take notes. We will build on this exercise in the next chapter.

---

[9] Breathing educator Patricia Gerbarg uses this "breath buddy" approach when working with children (https://www.breath-body-mind.com/berlin, 24 January 2022).

CHAPTER FOUR

Routines

Why do we make mistakes in performance even if we can play, sing or present without them in practice? How can we either release or work with and harness the tension that creeps in to find freedom, expression and joy in performance?

Seemingly inexplicable "choking" under pressure can happen to anyone, even professional musicians and athletes at the peak of their careers (Helding, 2020: 218). We will explore safety nets to solidify preparation and help minimise the risk of this happening in the next chapter. In this chapter, we will look at routines to support ourselves *before* the event and help achieve optimal performance states. We can implement these from several months or weeks to days or even moments before going on stage.

Top athletes use conditioned cues before competition (Clear, 2018: 132), while many professional musicians engage in ritualised behaviours to get into the right frame of mind before appearing in public (Helding, 2020: 249). The use of ritualised routines for the purpose of gathering and grounding is found in many traditions such as Japanese dance, martial arts and archery. Eugen Herrigel's beautiful book *Zen in the Art of Archery* provides a first-hand account of a Westerner discovering breathing and movement in preparation for releasing the arrow from the bow (see "Resources"). We can learn from the wisdom of ancient cultures and apply what we discover to contemporary contexts, using movement and breathwork to consciously calm SNS arousal.

I would like to remind you that this requires investment: we can't expect a quick fix with a short breathing exercise, magic meditation or movement sequence that we try for the first time before an important event. Instead, think of performance anxiety preparation in terms of self-care and continue stocking your sturdy shed with tools. It is important to create a personalised routine and do it regularly, ideally every day. This could be first thing in the morning, or before your musical or presentation time with just yourself as audience. That way, any interventions you select will feel familiar and create a sense of comfort when you use them before an actual performance. Try incorporating the following routines into your day and before you perform.

Movement

A few years ago, I had the fortune to work with James Britton, an osteopath whose patients include professional athletes, performers and musicians. James introduced me to the concept of the inseparable body and mind, the bo(dy-mi)nd, or "bond". He reminded me that when we are in the womb, our whole complex organism starts from simple cell division. James went on to explain that there isn't any separation between different organs, limbs and even the brain: just a process of differentiation and specialisation of tissues that change over time. This realisation helped me change the way I think about physical body sensations as well as thoughts and feelings such as anxiety: they are all interwoven and impossible to separate into distinct parts!

Movement can be extremely helpful for literally shifting internal states such as anxiety. When we feel anxious, it can be beneficial to "bypass" the mind by moving our body instead of trying to analyse or reason with what is happening. Movement takes us out of obsessive worrying. There is no need to implement a long or complex routine – just moving for a few minutes, or even 30 seconds, can be enough. Is your mind racing, getting caught up in worry loops? Take your attention out of these neural pathways and into the physical sensation of your body.

Movement also helps alleviate the SNS arousal symptoms of cold limbs and diverted blood flow. Combined with breathwork, it elicits PNS relaxation. Movement warms the body to reduce the risk of injury (by increasing blood flow to the muscles and tissues), releases physical tension, tones and conditions the heart, keeps joints healthy and increases circulation. From traditional healing perspectives of practices such as qigong and yoga, movement also encourages life force energy to circulate through the system (*qi* or *prana*), which ultimately improves overall health. According to naturopathic doctor, acupuncturist and practitioner of Chinese medicine Laurie Steelsmith, movement increases and balances the qi (Steelsmith, 2005: 37).

Intervention 1: Shake It!

This simple warm-up was taught by my late qigong master Jeff Cushing near the mountains of Snowdonia in North Wales. We would do the sequence every time to prepare the body for practising the forms. While related to martial arts traditions such as tai chi, qigong (pronounced chi kung) is primarily medicinal in nature. Translated as "energy work" or "breath work" (note the correspondence with the Sanskrit term *pranayama*, which is also linked to energy and the energetic principles of breathing), these practices work with subtle energy channels in the body, or meridians. In yoga terms, the equivalent channels are called *nadis*. When the meridians or *nadis* get blocked, energy stagnates, leading to feelings of unease and manifestation of disease.

You will need about a square metre of space, that's all – no yoga mat or specialist equipment (remember to check that the surface is non-slip and there are no sharp or breakable objects nearby). Alternatively, if you sit, choose a seat with no armrests. If standing, begin with your feet hip-width apart, toes pointing forwards and weight distributed equally between the four corners of each foot (if you are not sure about the distance, soften the knees and jump up and down a couple of times – where your feet land naturally is likely to be right for you). If you are sitting, make sure you are equally grounded through both sitting bones. You can do this short movement sequence on work breaks, first thing in the morning or whenever you need to shift your attention and focus and come back to the body.

Release your arms by your sides, soften the knees and gently shake out your hands through the fingers and wrists, being mindful of any injuries and listening to the body (as with any exercise, please stop or modify if something doesn't feel right). When you feel ready, invite the elbows to participate, finally releasing all the way from the shoulders down. Shift your weight from side to side as you shake: shaking to the left, shaking to the right. Notice your breathing: do you hold the breath when focusing on an unfamiliar task? Allow it to flow. Do this for a couple of minutes, then come to stillness.

When you stop, pause and notice how your body feels. Are there any residual sensations of movement? Tingling? Increased circulation? How is your breathing now?

For a more thorough warm-up, keep your knees soft and allow your arms to swing forwards and backwards like pendulums, assuming this is available and feels safe for your body. Let them be really relaxed and loose: see if it is possible not to "hold"

them at all. Feel yourself pushing the ground away
and imagine the movement initiating in the
foundations of the body. Notice what happens to the
top of your head. It might start moving up and down
– this vertical movement encourages the relaxed
swinging of the arms. You can also experiment with
swinging one arm forwards while the other one goes
backwards. After couple of minutes, allow the
movement to gradually subside and come to stillness,
noticing any sensations and your breathing as before.

Intervention 2: Short Breath Holds

Now that you are nicely warmed up, take a seat or lie
down in the same position as in Inquiry 3 (sitting
comfortably upright or lying on your back with the
knees bent and soles of the feet on the floor). If you
are seated, check that your knees are below your hips.
Bring your tongue to the roof of your mouth, as you
would to make a clucking sound. Allow the tongue to
curve and rest there. Let any tension in the jaw
release.

Notice your breathing yet again. What is the quality of
the breathing like – rough or smooth, deep or
shallow, long or short? What kind of texture and
rhythm does it have; what's the temperature of the
air? Which parts of the body is it felt in: the belly, the
chest, the ribcage, the back? Soften your belly,
allowing the movement to be felt there.

Take a normal breath in and out through the nose, without breathing in "extra" air to prepare. There is no need to try to breathe out all the air, either: just a normal exhale. After the exhale, hold the breath comfortably for 2-5 seconds (optionally, pinch your nose to ensure no extra air leaks in or out). Release the hold and inhale. Continue breathing normally through the nose for 10-15 seconds before doing another hold on the exhale. Repeat this five times and rest if you need to before doing another round. Do this exercise for 5 minutes at a time, up to once every hour if you have severe anxiety. This Oxygen Advantage® intervention is a traditional Buteyko method exercise, suitable as a warm-up before Intervention 3 below. It can also be used to reduce asthma symptoms or hyperventilation, ease congestion and constipation or even prevent a panic attack.

Intervention 3: Equal Wave Breath

This is a traditional yoga pranayama exercise that can be used to balance the two branches of the ANS, called Equal Wave or Equal Part Breath (*sama vritti* in Sanskrit). In yoga, our inhale is said to be linked with the energising / sympathetic response, and our exhale with the relaxing / parasympathetic. With this exercise, we are bringing the two "waves" into balance by making them the same length. At the same time, we slow down the air entering and leaving the lungs to send a message to the body-mind that everything is OK and build up precious CO_2 stores if they are depleted.

Calm breathing massages the vagus nerve through the diaphragm. The vagus ("wanderer" in Latin) runs through the major organs in the body, connecting the gut to the brain. It releases the neurotransmitter acetylcholine (ACh), which activates the parasympathetic response, slows down our heart rate and breathing and reduces inflammation (Rothenberg, 2020: 227). By controlling the breath, we also help optimise our heart rate variability (HRV). When we breathe in, the heart naturally speeds up slightly, slowing when we breathe out. A healthy range indicates more flexibility and resilience when it comes to dealing with stress (McKeown, 2021: 129).

Sitting or lying down as before in Inquiry 3 and Intervention 2, notice the quality of the natural breath again as you breathe in and out through your nose. Then, notice the length of the inhale and the exhale. Is one longer than the other, or are they approximately the same? Start gradually lengthening each breath in a soft and calm way. Remember, you are not necessarily taking in more air, but slowing and filtering the flow. If the inhale or the exhale is longer, gradually match them to be around the same length. This can be done intuitively or you can count the seconds, making each in- and out-breath last the same length of time: 4, 5 or 6 seconds (or whatever is comfortable for you).

Continue for a few breaths. If for any reason you are not comfortable, please feel free to return to Intervention 2 instead. Otherwise, if Equal Wave breathing feels OK – and you don't suffer from unregulated low or high blood pressure or heart problems, or are not in the first trimester of pregnancy – feel free to also experiment with introducing a tiny pause at the top of every inhale and the bottom of every exhale (*Kumbhaka*, or "breath retention" in Sanskrit). This can be 1, 2, or 3 seconds long. Eventually, you can aim to make the suspensions half the length of the breath (so, if you inhale for 6 seconds, hold for 3, exhale for 6, hold for 3). Continue for a few minutes, then allow your breathing to return to a natural rhythm. Notice how this makes you feel.

This "coherent" breathing rate of three to six breaths per minute is scientifically proven to synchronise oscillations in blood pressure with the rhythm of the heart. It also helps with healthy blood gas exchange and encourages relaxation through shifting us towards the PNS response (McKeown, 2021: 141)[10].

A guided video version of this exercise is available at https://xeniapestovabennett.com/videos (20 January 2022).

---

[10] Also known as "resonant breathing", the term "coherent breathing" is attributed to Stephen Elliott (https://coherentbreathing.org, 24 January 2022). Prominent teachers of this type of breathwork include Richard P. Brown and Patricia Gerbarg (https://www.breath-body-mind.com/about-bbm, 24 January 2022).

CHAPTER FIVE

Safety Nets

As soon as the external environment changes, the way we perform can also shift. This means that we need to have special security built in from the outset.

Safety nets can provide peace of mind and prevent things from becoming "unglued" should a hiccup happen in an unfamiliar situation. Having a roadmap helps – vocal coach and author Lynn Helding highlights the importance of building special cues into performance preparation to be able to continue even if things don't go according to plan (Helding, 2020: 217). We can also simulate things going wrong in the practice room and train ourselves to save the day by adjusting and adapting to the challenge. There are many different approaches to this kind of work. Here are a few suggestions from my personal arsenal for you to try.

Step One: Prepare the material for performance by making a grid of "salient points" (do this even if you perform from memory). In addition to working with sheet music, this step is applicable to a lead sheet, chord chart, structural outline, lyrics, a script for a presentation, a yoga sequence/lesson plan that you intend to teach, etc – adjust the exercise according to your needs. Analyse your material and identify sections that make structural sense. Make sure to clearly demarcate them. If you are a strongly visual person, you might find it helpful to use different colours – be creative (you can do this with a photocopy of the music if you don't want to deface the original, or consider using software on a tablet). It is important to make the sections short enough for your brain to be able to grasp them, yet to make sense within the narrative; this depends on the material.

Step Two: Try *starting* from the beginning of each section, stopping, then jumping to the next one. See if you can go through your material by iterating only the beginnings of each section, in order, training yourself not to search too long in between but to be able to jump quickly to the next convenient point on the grid. Stop randomly mid-phrase or mid-sentence and jump to the next convenient point without a gap, whether reading or by heart. Do this until it becomes second nature and you have the safety net firmly in place. The frequency of the starting points is up to you, but it is helpful if they are not too bitty, yet closely spaced enough to enable a coherent performance even if a chunk suddenly goes MIA.

If you perform with the score or read a script, beware: you might find yourself in an awkward position of having your material half-memorised. The danger here is that it can be easy to lose your place. Don't leave this to fate! Make sure to consciously decide which sections you will deliver completely by memory. Then, most importantly, mark a convenient place where you will come back to reading again, in a new colour or using a special sign, and work on *jumping directly to this section without a break* in case something does go wrong in the memorised section. As before, you can simulate this by stopping randomly a couple of times to test yourself and see if you are able to jump to the new starting point.

Visualisation is widely used by elite athletes and musicians. Depending on your goal, it can be employed at different stages of the preparation process. Visualisation helps internalise complex sections, strengthens memory, allows you to continue learning if you don't have access to a suitable instrument or space (such as when travelling or unwell), and conserves energy if you are recovering from injury or saving stamina and don't want to physically run through the performance many times on the same day.

Step One: While looking at the score/script, imagine performing *in real time* in your mind, without physically doing anything or making a sound. Do not make any movements – just sit comfortably somewhere quiet and calm. Picture as clearly as possible exactly what movements (and sounds) you would make: which finger is used when (it is very important to imagine correct fingering when visualising, or you will confuse your brain), how muscular engagement will be activated, how this will feel in the body. Imagine yourself noticing physical sensations in detail, as well as what you see (for example, keys under your fingers) and hear (not just pitch, but also intended dynamics and expression). This exercise can be difficult because we are not relying on the physical and auditory feedback we are used to. If you find that you just can't "see" certain parts or passages, isolate and practise these fuzzy sections "for real" (you can also work on visualising these passages slowly or with hands separately, if applicable). Gradually, the neural connections in your brain will get stronger. Start small: you can work this way with just a short chunk at a time, then build up. This exercise can be quite demanding at first, but is very much worth the investment!

Step Two: Imagine different performance situations and acoustics. This can, of course, be an actual upcoming performance, where you visualise in as much detail as possible the space, the audience and how you will feel backstage. Imagine everything going well – performance coach and author Vanessa Cornett encourages positive expectation combined with visualisation of what you will do before, during and after a performance (Cornett, 2019:130). You can also conjure up hypothetical environments and scenarios and adjust accordingly, while working with or away from your instrument. For example, which articulations, tempo and dynamics would you use if you suddenly found yourself in an enormous cathedral with long reverb? What about a really dry and lifeless studio? This is an approach taken by percussionist Evelyn Glennie, as discussed in her interview with performance anxiety coach Charlotte Tomlinson[11]. Work to be able to perform each piece at different speeds to adjust to acoustics. You can also ask yourself how will you keep going if someone in the audience is constantly shuffling, sniffing, coughing, unwrapping sweets or dropping their keys?

---

[11] Available at http://www.beyondstagefright.com/evelyn-glennie/, 11 January 2022.

This is just one very common scenario in a performance situation.

Intervention 4: Rotations

Revisit the movement sequence from Intervention 1 (shaking from the shoulders and swinging the arms to release tension). Once you are nicely warmed up, start slowly rotating through the shoulders backwards a few times; you can bring your fingertips to the top of the shoulder or even extend the arms without locking the elbows if that feels nice (however, please remember to take into account any pre-existing injuries or conditions). A guided video version of these exercises is available at https://xeniapestovabennett.com/videos (20 January 2022).

We often mis-map our shoulders and their range of motion in our minds. When asked where their arm attaches to the body, many of my students point at the tip of their shoulder. This is not true. The whole shoulder girdle is attached to the torso at the breastbone through the sternoclavicular joint. You can feel this attachment by following along your clavicle, or collarbone, to the centre – this little connection holds your whole arm! The collarbone is also very mobile, helping the whole range by lifting when necessary. It can move up, down, forward, back and rotate (Mark, 2003: 71).

With your elbows softly bent at your sides, turn your torso left to right a few times, leading from the belly button to warm up the spine. Next, try hip circles: place your hands on your hips or the small of your back and rotate in one direction, starting small and gradually increasing your range, if that feels OK. Imagine that you are stirring and scraping the sides of a big pot. Switch direction, again starting small and gradually increasing if this feels good for your body.

Finally, a different swinging arms exercise. Standing relaxed with the feet hip-width apart, point your belly button to the left, then to the right as you initiate rotation on this plane. Keep the knees soft and the arms completely loose: eventually, the arms will follow the body as you increase momentum, swinging around by themselves like a propeller. It's important to remain relaxed – you are not "making" the arms move. Think of the movement as originating in the belly, in the core, the gravity centre of your being. Add a little dip in the knees as you turn side to side, allowing the top of the head to move up and down and your arms to flop and slap wherever they like to release tension in the upper back and the trapezius. Take your time to explore this relaxing movement. Then, gradually decrease the range, slowly coming to stillness. Notice how your body is feeling now: are there any sensations of tingling, pulsing, vibration, circulation, internal motion?

If you suffer from dry mouth when anxious, you can add a tongue rotation exercise at the end to encourage saliva production. Keeping your mouth closed, swirl the tip of the tongue around the front in circles a few times in one direction, then the other direction. Swallow and notice how it feels (thank you to Alexander Technique teacher Penny O'Connor for sharing this gem).

Inquiry 4: Visualisation with Equal Wave Breath

Sitting or lying down comfortably, bring your tongue to the roof of your mouth and allow it to relax, softening the jaw and opening the airways. Visualise a recent/upcoming/imaginary performance with as much clarity as possible. This can be the same scenario you used in Inquiry 1, or a different one. Notice any sensations and symptoms of anxiety that might come up. Try not to react or tighten against these, but become aware of them, acknowledge them, say "hello". Pay attention to your breath and heart rate. Activate Equal Wave Breath for a few minutes (if this is difficult, please use Short Breath Holds instead). Visualise the same scenario again after breathing and notice how you feel. Take notes. Eventually, you can try doing the breathing exercise *while* visualising.

As a next step, consider going out for a walk and activating Equal Parts Breath when the heart rate is gently elevated. You can also do this during yoga or any other mild physical activity. It is possible to calm the breath and keep the inhale and exhale slow even if the heart is beating a little bit faster. This is an interesting practice to play with to simulate what you can do before an actual performance.

CHAPTER SIX

Focus and Anxiety

When I was designing the *Befriending Performance Anxiety* course, I interviewed a number of non-professional musicians as part of my research. I specifically sought people who were doing music in their spare time. Increasing resources are now offered to professionals-in-training through educational institutions as well as excellent organisations such as BAPAM[12], but I wanted to know what sort of help was available to those outside these networks. I was also keen to find out about their feelings surrounding performance anxiety. One of the questions I asked was: what would happen if you could wave a magic wand, and your performance anxiety would suddenly disappear?[13]

---

[12] British Association for Performing Arts Medicine offers free workshops and individual sessions to support musicians' health (see "Resources").

[13] I borrowed this strategy from author and coach Amanda Cook, whose courses and books continue to inspire thousands: https://amandacook.me, 11 January 2022.

The answers ranged from feeling more confident and releasing inhibition to discovering pride, achievement, freedom, not worrying about what people think, finding joy in playing for others, feeling "absolutely brilliant", "being over the moon", "jumping up and down with joy", feeling empowered and being more honest about who they are. Many interviewees also felt these changes would spill over into areas of their lives beyond music-making.

While we have no magic wand and performance anxiety is a long-term project, we can still work with these powerful goals to help anchor motivation and build focus. In this chapter, we will look at ways to strengthen and train attention. We will also explore different types of focus to perform at our best.

Training Attention through Mindfulness

Remember the "befriending" concept from the Introduction? When we befriend difficulty, we become aware of discomfort, looking at it instead of pushing it away. Practices that cultivate mindful attention train us to learn to feel tension or performance anxiety and identify these symptoms as sensations, thoughts and emotions (see the interventions at the end of this chapter). Researcher and mindfulness teacher Jon Kabat-Zinn shares the following:

 (Kabat-Zinn, 1990: 338).

F.M. Alexander, the creator of the Alexander Technique, likened performance anxiety to *habitual* response to stimuli. The question to ask is whether we wish to continue indulging in old habits, reinforcing the same neural pathways, or choose to observe and not react in predictable ways, building new connections in the brain instead. Becoming aware of physical as well as psychological habits is the first step on our journey. We can start by simply noticing reaction patterns: what happens in the body-mind? Do I tense my neck or jaw, do I raise my shoulders when I am anxious? Specific tension can be diffused "indirectly" through using our senses and noticing whatever else is going on in the system instead of focusing further on the problem in a narrow way and amplifying it (Kleinman and Buckoke, 2015: 248). In other words, we can reduce reactivity, choosing how to respond in any given moment – but this is something that needs to be trained.

Focus in Performance

During my interviews, one recurring theme was "focus": how do we maintain focus in performance? Many of us find our mind wandering and drifting off, leading to near-catastrophic results. We try harder and tense up even further, metaphorically "gripping" every note, if we are musicians. Control and accuracy continue to elude us in this situation. It is almost as if the harder we try, the worse we perform.

As well as interpreting the word "focus" as concentration, we can think of it more as our field of vision. When we are in SNS mode, our field of vision narrows to pinpoint whatever is most important (this is also what happens when we spend most of our day staring at screens). Opening peripheral vision can help alleviate this tension. Taking breaks to look around is invaluable – going outside, walking in nature (or a park for city-dwellers) and looking at the distant horizon does wonders for stress reduction.

In performance, the tendency to be hypervigilant and narrow our vision affects the way we use our attention. It is important to remember the difference between practice and performance. One of my piano teachers Philip Mead used to remind me that when we work on a piece or passage in our own time, we are constantly looking *backwards* at what went wrong so that we can stop and fix it. When we are performing, we can't afford to slow down and look back, analysing mistakes – we need to remain present in the moment. If anything, we also continuously look *forwards* to what's coming next in the music if reading from the score. This approach requires a gear shift of mindset and really helps maintain focus.

As noted by Alexander, the field of vision also connects to the level of tension in the body and can impact the quality of performance, slowing us down as we "grab" every note or word in narrow focus attention if reading. To counter this, we can learn to widen out to "panoramic vision", a term attributed to Alexander technique and vision specialist Peter Grunwald and applied to performance contexts by Judith Kleinman and Peter Buckoke (Kleinman and Buckoke, 2015: 120). According to the authors, over-focusing and fixing the eyes also restricts breathing and slows down reading. If you feel stuck in this way, you can briefly look into the distance (such as above your music stand) then return to your immediate surroundings in close-up to reboot the system (ibid: 125). This is also an excellent trick when working at the computer.

Researcher Les Fehmi takes the concept of peripheral spatial awareness even further. Fehmi writes about athletes and musicians as erroneously thinking that:

...THE HARDER THEY PUSH, THE BETTER THEY WILL PERFORM. BUT THAT IS OFTEN NOT THE CASE. RATHER, EVERYONE NEEDS TO KNOW WHEN TO PUSH HARD AND WHEN NOT TO, WHEN TO NARROW FOCUS AND WHEN TO USE DIFFUSE OR OTHER STYLES OF ATTENTION. THOSE WHO PERFORM ONLY IN NARROW FOCUS ARE OFTEN "HYPER-FOCUSED" AND WASTE MUCH ENERGY FIGHTING THEIR OWN TENSE, OVERLY EXCITED PHYSIOLOGY, WHICH

FURTHER INCREASES MUSCLE TENSION AND RAISES HEART AND RESPIRATORY RATES. THESE PROBLEMS OFTEN WORSEN DURING COMPETITION, WHEN FOCUS NARROWS EVEN FURTHER. NARROW FOCUS ALSO *ENGENDERS PERFORMANCE ANXIETY* (Fehmi, 2007: 114, emphasis mine).

Fehmi urges us to release muscle tone by diffusing attention equally throughout the body instead:

MOST OF US… ARE UNWITTINGLY CLUNKING AROUND IN A KIND OF BODY ARMOUR, OUR MUSCLES HABITUALLY TENSED… UNCONSCIOUSLY HELD MUSCLE TENSION REQUIRES SYMPATHETIC AUTONOMIC ACTIVATION, YIELDING ANXIETY, INCREASED HEART RATE, AND DRAINED ENERGY RESOURCES… (Ibid: 117).

So, somewhat counter-intuitively, you might find that you are able to focus better if you consciously relax and open awareness to your peripheral vision while becoming aware of whatever else is happening in and around your space. The interventions at the end of this chapter provide some guidance, as do the breathing and movement exercises that we explore throughout this book.

Intervention 5: Breath and Movement (Take a Break!)

Slow and mindful movement linked with breathwork can be profoundly beneficial for eliciting the relaxation response. This is also an excellent intervention if you need to take a break from your computer screen or practice session, widen peripheral awareness and look beyond what is directly in front of you, literally and metaphorically.

Begin by warming up with shaking and joint rotations as in Interventions 1 and 4. When you feel ready, interlace your hands and face the palms outwards. Keeping the elbows soft and being careful not to lock the joints or tense the neck, reach up over head as you breathe in calmly through the nose. Leave space between the shoulders and the ears, keeping the neck long. Turn to twist to the right as you breathe out through the nose. Inhale to centre, exhale to the left. Repeat once or twice.

Release the hands and clasp them again, but with the other thumb on top – this might feel unusual. Inhaling as you reach the arms up towards the ceiling once more, this time fold to the right as you exhale, stretching the left side body, being mindful not to overextend. Come up to centre as you inhale and fold to the left, stretching the right side as you exhale again. Repeat. Release the arms and give them a little shake.

Next, face your palms up around hip-height and softly arch your arms as if you are holding a very large bowl or beach ball. Keep the knees soft. Breathing in slowly through the nose, bring the hands up to about chest height. Turn the palms to face the floor and lower them towards the pelvis as you exhale (still breathing through the nose). Continue with this slow mindful movement for about 10 cycles, linking it with the breath: up on the inhale, down on the exhale. The slower you move, the slower you breathe – aim to make the inhale and exhale approximately the same length (this is our Equal Wave Breath in motion). This qigong exercise is traditionally used to balance liver energy and is excellent for calming down when feeling stressed, anxious or angry. It is also helpful when getting ready for sleep. A guided video version of these exercises is available at https://xeniapestovabennett.com/videos (20 January 2022).

Finish by "sweeping" the energy to your lower belly centre three times: inhale as you lift the arms overhead and bring the hands down slowly as you exhale, with your palms gliding down above an imaginary central line about an inch away from the front of the body.

Intervention 6: Grounding Motivation Focus

This meditation is an adaptation of "Arriving and Centering" by Sarah Powers (Powers, 2008: 179). It encourages us to connect with our intention and reasons for doing something, energising commitment.

Sitting comfortably on a chair or meditation cushion with your weight equally distributed between the left and right as well as front and back, keep your spine relaxed but long and place your hands in your lap (you can also do this exercise lying down or standing). Lower the gaze or allow the eyes to close softly. Start with a short mental body scan to release any pockets of tension that you become aware of, from the top of the head melting down the face, throat, back of the head, neck, shoulders, arms and hands, chest and belly, back, pelvis, legs and feet. Allow any tension to trickle down into the ground.

Become aware of your feet on the ground and your sitting bones on the chair or cushion. Notice your breathing: the air gently flowing in and out through the nostrils, the movement of the body breathing, soft expansion of the belly and movement of the ribs with every inhale. Place your attention into your belly, the gravity centre of your body. Try to soften it somewhat to allow the breath to reside there. Known as the "belly brain", our gut has more nerves than the spinal cord and produces 90% of the serotonin in the body (the chemical that stabilises our mood, Rothenberg, 2020: 250). In ancient healing and martial arts, this region has enormous significance and is a seat of energy and power. Remember the swinging arms exercise where you initiated movement from the belly, with the arms following? Called the *Dan Tien* in Daoist arts or *Hara* in Japanese traditions, this energetic plexus is where effortless movement and confidence originate from (see "Resources" for a wonderful classic text by Karlfried Graf Dürckheim on this subject).

Connect with and remind yourself of your motivation. Why are you reading this book? Why are you committed to finding ways to befriend performance anxiety? What is it that drives you forward – what do you love about performing? I take a moment to do this short grounding exercise and remind myself of my motivation every time I sit down at the piano, whether it is to play for myself or for others. My primary motivation is my love of music. Firstly, I do it for myself. Secondly, I do it to share with others. What is your motivation? Hold on to it and use it to energise your commitment!

A guided audio version of this intervention is available at https://xeniapestovabennett.com/bellybrain/ (20 January 2022).

Intervention 7: Open Focus

Traditional Insight Meditation approaches can help build resilience and non-reactivity. They also train concentration and encourage the widening of awareness to incorporate different elements of what is going on, counteracting the fight-or-flight tunnel vision effect. You can do this simple exercise before/during performing, as well as first thing in the morning or whenever you feel you need it.

Sitting, standing or lying down comfortably, start with a short mental body scan. Notice *sensations* in your body (tingling, pressure of the seat against the chair, itching, throbbing, clothes on your skin, pain, heat, temperature of the air). Next, acknowledge any thoughts, coming and going. As well as thoughts, can you expand your field of awareness to incorporate any feelings without running away with them? They might be pleasant, unpleasant or neutral (looking forward to or dreading something yet to come, pleased with or annoyed at something that happened earlier, feeling relaxed, feeling anxious, feeling sleepy or bored). Lastly, expand awareness to incorporate anything you hear – sounds around or outside the space. Allow awareness of these different senses to interweave with each other, come to the fore and back away. If you find yourself getting carried away with one more than the others, notice "what else is going on" in and around the body and remind yourself to expand attention from narrow to wide focus. Stay in this open, non-judgemental space for 6-12 minutes before continuing with your day.

You can also enhance this Mindful Focus exercise by incorporating spatial awareness. Penny O'Connor offers an excellent guided audio version of the Balanced Resting State, available at https://www.alexanderpen.co.uk/about-the-alexander-technique/the-balanced-resting-state/ (11 January 2022).

CHAPTER SEVEN

Improvisation in Life and Art

The title of this chapter is taken from *Free Play: Improvisation in Life and Art*, a wonderful book by viola player Stephen Nachmanovitch (see "Resources"). This book was passed around among friends while I was an undergraduate student in piano performance and composition many years ago. Everyone was invited to underline passages that were relevant to them. By the time we were finished, virtually the entire book was full of lines, doodles and scribbles. Free Play is an attitude that allows us to look at life as a creative act. Whether making music or performing in any other way, we are free to explore and experiment, discovering like children and embracing spontaneity. No matter how much preparation we put in before a performance, we can't predict every situation that might arise. The sooner we make peace with this, the quicker we can move on to putting our energy into performing rather than worrying about it. In fact, things going wrong might not necessarily be all bad!

Some of my clients are non-professional musicians who are highly accomplished in their fields. They are often comfortable with and used to speaking in public, feeling confident standing up in front of large groups of strangers. They regularly present in high-stakes situations such as board meetings or sales pitches. However, some of them still find it incredibly difficult to perform in a musical capacity for friends and family. Why?

In addition to perhaps not exposing themselves to this mode of performance as often, one reason could be that if they stumble slightly when speaking, they know how to "improvise", provided the topic is familiar. In this situation, it is always possible to take a micro-pause and recalibrate, gathering thoughts as we take a breath or a sip of water.

This is obviously different in a performance situation when we are presenting fixed material, such as a pre-composed piece of music, either by memory or from the score. Or... is it?

Many of us are brought up as perfectionists and fear judgement from others while judging ourselves. Undoubtedly, this is something that you are familiar with if you are reading this book. When performing creatively, we also tend to assume that every audience member is as intimately familiar with the material as we are, and has a critical outlook. The reality is that this is simply not true. Even on rare occasions when someone follows the score during performance, it is highly unlikely that they will spot every tiny mistake.

In fact, the old saying of "fake it till you make it" very much applies here. The art of stagecraft dictates that while on stage, we are acting a part. If we appear confident and keep going, 90% of the audience will not notice even if something goes wrong – provided we don't stop. However, it can be tempting to sabotage the performance by grimacing, tutting or otherwise giving away when something doesn't go according to plan, drawing attention to it. This is common among my less experienced university students. They feel that they are somehow being inauthentic if they don't acknowledge their imperfections. They might sigh, roll their eyes or restart passages, making it obvious to the listener that they made a mistake. Try video recording yourself to check if you have these habits. While it is easy to grasp that this is not ideal on an intellectual level, it can take some work to undo.

However, let's assume you can already keep a poker face when something goes wrong. What if, despite your preparation, you have a memory blank or lose your place on the page? What if anxiety hits unexpectedly, and you start feeling less in control, experiencing symptoms such as shaking? Again, simply continue faking it, making some sort of sound or movement to keep going until your brain comes back online and you can jump back onto your safety net grid from Chapter 5.

Becoming more comfortable with the concept of improvisation helps. Everyone can improvise. We can simply think of improvisation as "making noises". Free improvisation doesn't have to be in a stylistically appropriate idiom; you are just aiming to be able to keep going until you can jump back to where you are meant to be. Subscribe to the philosophical approach of the American composer John Cage: any sound can be musical – it's how you listen to it. Have a go at the following intervention to start cultivating spontaneous performance.

Intervention 8: Free Play

Step One: Be kind to yourself and accept that you *will* make mistakes. Let go of rigidity. There is no way around it – you will not be "perfect" in every performance (whatever that means, anyway), and ultimately that's fine. Try lowering imaginary and unrealistic standards and allow things to happen, good as well as bad. You might discover spontaneous new ways of interpreting a familiar piece of music, a different sound or way of shaping a phrase.

Step Two: Building from Chapter 5, revise your safety net grid points to jump to in your chosen presentation material. The next time you go through in the practice room, try interrupting the flow on purpose (as if something went wrong in performance). This time, before jumping to the next point, see if you can improvise for a few seconds by simply "making noises" to keep going for a while. This can be some sort of riffing in the same key (if appropriate), but also anything at all – whatever is under your fingers or whatever comes out! Think of it as giving your brain a chance to recalibrate, as you would if you were giving a lecture and took a moment to clear your throat. Then, jump to the next grid point. See what happens: even if it sounds awful for a few seconds, there is a good chance that people won't notice or will forget about it if you keep going as if nothing happened. Remain confident – you will be pleasantly surprised at how little of what you think is terrible people take in.

Additional Support: If the concept of improvisation is completely new to you, text scores and graphic scores are a fun starting point. These ways of making music and art allow us to become childlike again, approaching creativity with an open and uninhibited innocence that is often missing from our adult lives. Playing with sounds and movements like toys can be incredibly liberating. Making deliberately non-musical noises with instruments or objects (music boxes, mechanical gadgets or anything that makes a sound) and learning to structure and perceive these in musical ways are excellent training tools. Try the suggestions below for ideas and inspiration (see "Resources" for book details).

Pauline Oliveros: *Sonic Meditations* (https://monoskop.org/images/0/09/Oliveros_Pauli ne_Sonic_Meditations_1974.pdf, 11 January 2022): *A classic collection of text scores encouraging intuition and communication from a pioneer of "deep listening". Accessible to all levels of ability, musicians and non-musicians alike, requiring nothing but an open mind.*

Randy Raine-Reusch: Selection of Graphic Scores
(available at https://www.asza.com/r3sc.shtml, 11
January 2022): *This beautiful collection of free graphic
scores opens a door to a new world: the delicate images
are inspired by Japanese brushstrokes, at times featuring
elements of standard notation as well as verbal
instructions to realisation. There is no right or wrong,
just fun exploration.*

Jonathan Burrows: *A Choreographer's Handbook*
(Routledge): *This is a gem of an inspiring book, full of
ideas on preparing and structuring a performance in any
medium. A real creative block-buster!*

John Lely and James Saunders: *Word Events:
Perspectives on Verbal Notation* (Bloomsbury): *A
thorough companion to text scores with many weird and
wonderful examples included.*

Michael Nyman: *Experimental Music: Cage and Beyond*
(Schirmer Books): *An introduction to the older
generation of experimental composers, including some
text scores that are fun to realise.*

CHAPTER EIGHT

Post–Performance

Throughout this book, we have been exploring tools and approaches to use before and during your performance. In this chapter, we will look at routines to employ *after* performing. We tend to forget about the post-performance wind-down, too stressed or elated to think about it. However, this is as important as your pre-performance support in order to maximise the success of subsequent events. Let's explore strategies to help you physically and mentally after the challenge of getting up in front of people.

Physical Support

We know that physical warm-up exercises can help to prepare the body for performance while also supporting performance anxiety (see Chapter 4). Movement is also great afterwards. A post-performance routine releases stress hormones that may have accumulated and floods the body with endorphins. Exercise is ideal for this, but not only the active cardiovascular types. More calming styles of movement, such as tai chi, qigong and yoga, are wonderful for calming down post-performance as well as counteracting the generally hectic pace of our lives. Even slower practices, such as Yin or Restorative yoga, are also excellent for eliciting the relaxation response. According to wellness coach Aimee Hartley, held forward-folds can be very helpful to wind down before sleep (Hartley, 2020: 76, see Intervention 9 at the end of this chapter).

Experimenting with stillness and postural support in an Alexander Technique semi-supine constructive rest position is another excellent way to balance and reset the whole system (see the Balanced Resting State exercise link at the end of Chapter 6).

We can also implement specific breathing techniques that have a soothing effect. Learning to breathe lower into the lungs and slowing the flow of air while lengthening the exhale has a calming energetic quality. The Humming Bee Breath exercise at the end of this chapter is proven to increase relaxation and improve healthy cardiovascular resting patterns while also restoring CO_2 levels to a healthy balance (Rothernberg, 2020: 230).

Psychological Support: Working with Rewards

Remember the importance of looking forwards to what is coming in the music (or text) when performing from Chapter 6? As well as literally looking ahead to the material we are about to present, we can also look forward to a *reward*. Decide ahead of time how you will treat yourself for rising to the challenge of performing.

Research in neuroscience points to neuroplasticity, the possibility to rewire our brains through encouraging ourselves with rewards. It is the anticipation rather than fulfilment that motivates us to take action (Clear, 2018: 106). This is different from going for addictive hits of dopamine by constantly seeking external praise and validation from others. Instead, try shifting the focus to congratulating yourself for small achievements. Setting up, acknowledging and celebrating even small milestones is an effective way to enjoy more aspects of performing (Cornett, 2019: 40, 232). In general, "carrots" are also much more efficient than "sticks" when we are building up the motivation to do something (Peters, 2012: 261). Think about the types of carrots you can set up for yourself in the inquiry below.

Inquiry 5: Positive Reward Mechanisms

When I was a postgraduate student at the Conservatory of Amsterdam, my fellow piano classmate and friend Ermis Theodorakis had an unconventional learning style. Blessed with incredible memory and visual capacity, Ermis was able to learn a complex musical score without once trying it at the piano. He would sit in his living room, switch on MTV for "light entertainment" (those were the days!) and pore over ultra-complex compositions by Iannis Xenakis and Claus-Steffen Mahnkopf, figuring out overlaid rhythms and committing the material to memory. During subsequent performances, Ermis would use his strongly visual imagination to clearly "see" the score as well as a large picture of a beer mug etched onto the last page of the music in his mind's eye. This gave him the impetus to keep going and look forward to a reward at the end. I recently asked Ermis if this visualisation is still important to him, twenty years on. He writes:

(correspondence with the author, 14 December 2021).

Of course, I am not advocating alcohol or cigars as a reward, so ask yourself, what could this be for you? Take a moment to think of positive mechanisms to treat yourself after an upcoming performance, no matter how big or small. Could it be a nice bubble bath, a yummy treat, something that really supports and nourishes the whole system such as a relaxing massage, a soothing yoga session, a lovely bit of stretching and breathwork? Or maybe a bigger reward, like going away somewhere nice for the weekend? Jot down ideas.

Intervention 9: Post-Performance Stretching

This can also be great after a practice session or between bouts of working at the computer. Begin with the Breath and Movement intervention from Chapter 6. Follow with chest-opener stretches: resting one hand against a wall with your thumb pointing up, extend the arm as you turn to face the opposite direction from your fingers, opening across the chest. Hold comfortably for about 30 seconds and repeat on the other side. Alternatively, do both sides at once by standing in a doorway with your arms extended, walking forwards between them until you feel a comfortable stretch (be careful not to over-extend the joints, especially if you are hyper-mobile).

Balance chest-openers with a held yin yoga forward-fold. Sitting in a chair or on the ground with your hips elevated on a folded blanket or cushion, stretch your legs out in front of you; feel free to slightly bend the knees and support your hamstrings with further padding, such as another rolled-up blanket, scarf or jumper, if that is more comfortable. You can remain upright, leaning on your fingertips behind you to keep the spine long, if that provides enough of a stretch; or start folding from the hips as you walk your hands forwards. Allow gravity to do the work without pulling or forcing. Again, feel free to use whatever support is handy – a cushion or pillow under your belly or a yoga bolster to support the forehead can feel very comforting. Don't allow the head to dangle unsupported for too long: extend the back of the neck and micro-tuck the chin, keeping the neck in line with the rest of the spine. Hold this pose for 1-5 minutes as gravity gently loads and tugs on the deep tissues in the body, breathing softly in and out through the nose, and optionally activating your Equal Wave Breath from Chapter 4.

Intervention 10: Humming Bee Breath

"Brahmari" is an ancient yogic practice. It really sounds like a droning beehive when you get this going with a group of people in the same space! Elongating the exhale helps activate the PNS relaxation response, while humming encourages the production of nitric oxide in our nasal cavities (an important signalling molecule that acts as an antiviral and antimicrobial and encourages healthy circulation).

Take a comfortable calm breath in through the nose and exhale slowly as you relax the throat, gently humming a low pitch with your mouth closed for as long as your breath lasts. There is no need to hum loudly or for a particularly long time: we are not singing. For the record, I have successfully done this exercise on the noisy Northern Line of the London Underground many times without anyone noticing! Try cupping your ears with your hands to feel vibrations in the skull as you hum. Repeat 15 times or more to fully benefit from the relaxing effect of lengthening the exhale.

A guided video version of this exercise is available at https://xeniapestovabennett.com/videos (20 January 2022).

CHAPTER NINE

Exposure Therapy

We've now looked at what we can do before, during and after performing to support our experience and preparation. Hopefully, you've already been trying out the movement, breathing and focus exercises to see which ones resonate with you and can work as part of a regular routine. It is now time to put the theory into practice. This chapter provides the most important exercise of the book: don't skip it and don't delay on implementing the practical experience!

Establishing Safe Spaces

Having goals to aim for is very helpful for motivation. Exposure therapy, a type of behavioural therapy, is a researched treatment for performance anxiety alongside some of the other techniques we have explored so far including approaches based on yoga, mindfulness and Alexander Technique (Helding, 2020: 227). However, it is also important not to jump in the deep end too soon: establish safe control settings first. What kinds of situations could provide you with that little adrenaline boost without major pressure? Is there a comfortable halfway point that will allow you to get a taste of managing SNS arousal as you build up to more challenging performance scenarios?

Performing online for a small group or inviting just one or two friends or family members can provide a perfect "safe space". Performing also becomes easier if you do a little "tour" of the same material in a limited space of time. This takes the pressure off individual events – you don't need to worry about a single performance being the definitive version if you have several lined up, giving you opportunities to test approaches, gradually iron out insecurities or technical weaknesses and see what works best. From my experience, having several performances in a row is the best way to secure material (five to eight over the course of two to four weeks works well – I am rarely relaxed the very first time I play something in public).

Consider booking a mini-series of performances for yourself, online and/or in person for family and friends. Choose one or two items to start with rather than a whole programme and present these over the course of several weeks. Practise the interventions and make sure to prepare treats for afterwards. You will start feeling more relaxed and be able to perform more accurately and more expressively. This will help you build confidence and enjoy playing for others more. Remember to be kind to yourself and build up slowly, starting with small audiences and short presentations.

Connection

In his fascinating book *The Body Keeps the Score*, Bessel van der Kolk describes the brain as a "cultural organ", shaped through experience of interacting with others (see "Resources"). Social engagement is paramount for humans – we are "built" to register facial expressions and perceive safety and danger through interaction and communication. Social support and supportive relationships help release stress, shifting us out of fight-or-flight.

We were painfully reminded of this need for connection during times of profound isolation in the Covid-19 lockdowns. Establishing and nurturing a sense of community is extremely important to support performance anxiety management. The one thing that becomes apparent to participants on the *Befriending Performance Anxiety* course is how much we all have in common: our love of performance as well as our anxiety symptoms, wobbles and doubts. These worries and responses are what makes us human. Sharing experiences allows participants to connect and realise this.

You can build your own connectivity and community by linking up with other performers who have similar concerns, either in person or online. For musicians, this can be through your local music teacher organisation or your instrument or voice association. Performing regularly for each other is extremely beneficial, not only through providing goals and accountability, but also by learning from each other.

These people become your "tribe": they know what you are going through and can share their own tips and tricks as well as create a safe and supportive environment to experiment in.

Our regular online performance forum is free and open to all on a first-come, first-served basis (not only professional and non-professional musicians, but also lecturers, yoga teachers and all other performing practitioners). You can find out about and register for upcoming sessions by joining the mailing list in "Resources".

Intervention 11: Putting it all Together

Step One: Arrive. Sitting down comfortably, prepare for planning your tour. Notice any feelings of apprehension, sensations of anxiety manifesting, doubting thoughts, physical tension. Invite them to stay without fighting them; explore them in a friendly and open way.

Connect to the ground under your feet, the grounding presence of your breath, wherever it is felt the most at the moment, the belly-brain centre. Become aware of sensations in your body, thoughts as they come up without running away with them, feelings, sounds.

The reason for doing this kind of work is to train yourself to notice any disturbing thoughts or sensations before or during performance and acknowledge them instead of fighting, then move back to the task. You can diffuse anxious feelings without focusing on them by allowing awareness of what else is going on to be present. I feel churning in my stomach, OK, how is the breathing? What else is happening – is there any tension I can release in the body? How about my vision, is it narrow – can I widen peripheral awareness or look over the music stand momentarily then come back to resettle myself? This helps concentration by staying *out of the head* and in the body instead of losing focus, spacing out or engaging in worrying, negative or panicky thoughts.

Step Two: Anchor in Motivation. Remind yourself again of your motivation for performing. What are some of the positive feelings that you can enjoy through sharing with others? What if you had that magic wand and were able to fast-track the befriending experience – how would you feel? Why are you interested and committed; what are you most looking forward to? What rewards will you set up for yourself? How will you wind down afterwards? How about further performance opportunities that you can set up and look forward to? Take notes.

Step Three: Breathe. Become aware of your breathing, wherever it is felt in the body, just as it is, without modifying it for now. It could be the belly expanding and releasing, the ribs moving out sideways with every inhale and returning with every exhale, the cooler temperature of the air coming into the nostrils, the warmer flow leaving them. Stay with this awareness for a while. This traditional mindfulness exercise is called *Anapanasati* in Pali and was taught by the Buddha. It trains the mind to stay concentrated on one task without distraction. Sooner or later, we might get waylaid by thoughts, feelings and sounds. Unlike in the wider focus of Insight Meditation (Intervention 7), here we simply bring our attention back to the breath. It will take some training and regular practice, but the payoff is worth the effort. You can stay with this attention exercise for a couple of minutes to start with and gradually increase to 6 or 12 minutes, building up to longer periods over time. Set a timer to help you.

Feel free to finish the intervention here and go on to the planning stage below. Alternatively, continue with Short Breath Holds and/or Equal Wave Breath.

Step Four: Let's Plan! Now it's time to commit to your goals. Set down realistic and achievable but exciting and challenging deadlines for yourself. How many concert "tour" dates would you like to do, and when? How will you deliver these – in person or online? Put your dates in your calendar and let your invited audience know as soon as possible so that you have someone to account to. Don't forget to decide on your pre- and post-performance routines as well as which rewards you will set up. Then, reward yourself for doing this exercise!

FINAL THOUGHTS

Moving Forward

We have come to the end of our journey together for now. Revisit Inquiry 1 from Chapter Two. How do you feel about your performance anxiety now? Is it possible to observe it in a less reactive, more open, compassionate and curious way? In Internal Family Systems Therapy, Schwartz lists eight qualities of relating to parts from one's centre, the *Self* with a capital S rather than from another part, all beginning with the letter C: *Curiosity, Calm, Confidence, Connectedness, Clarity, Creativity, Courage* and *Compassion* (Schwartz and Sweezy, 2020: 49). These provide a helpful compass system for our progress as we befriend our performance anxiety.

Consider the possibility that performance anxiety symptoms are messages for positive change. Are there better ways to take care of your physical and mental needs, including general health and stress management? Could some of the tools we've been exploring in this book help nourish and nurture your rest and recovery time as well as encourage you to exercise more? Is it possible to imagine sensations and feelings associated with being nervous eventually

adding energy, zest and excitement to performance?
Take a moment to write down ideas and sum up
approaches that you can add to your personal tool
shed.

I hope that this selection of strategies and
interventions to use before, during and after
performing resonated with you and will ease your
befriending process. You will find that some of the
exercises have an immediate effect, while others
require a little more investment to feel comfortable
and familiar. Take good care of the tools in your shed:
you will also discover others to add to this collection
as your expertise and comfort levels grow.

There are many more techniques to explore. If you
would like to be guided through the interventions and
learn about other topics, including nutrition for
anxiety and working with our inner critic voices,
please consider joining the *Befriending Performance
Anxiety* course. You are also very welcome to sign up
for our free events and performance forums; please
see the list of "Resources" below.

Thank you for reading this book! I wish you a fruitful
relationship with your creativity in performance and
look forward to connecting again soon.

Dr Xenia Pestova Bennett, January 2022

OPEN SPACE

Use these pages to take notes on your experience and write down ideas.

____

____

____

____

____

____

Online Resources

Bonus book materials (breathing and movement exercise videos, breathing exercise positions, guided relaxation audio): access at
https://xeniapestovabennett.com/resources

Befriending Performance Anxiety online course and links to Xenia's other writings:
https://xeniapestovabennett.com/perform

Mailing List: join our community of like-minded performers to receive invitations to free events and the online performance forum:
https://tinyurl.com/befriendinganxiety

Xenia's Breathing Classes:
https://xeniapestovabennett.com/wellbeing/breath

Xenia's Yoga Classes and Yoga Mindset Coaching:
https://xeniapestovabennett.com/wellbeing/yoga-coaching

British Association for Performing Arts Medicine:
https://www.bapam.org.uk

More information on the Oxygen Advantage®:
https://oxygenadvantage.com

Oxygen Advantage® method instructors by area:
https://oxygenadvantage.com/instructors/

Penny O'Connor's Balanced Resting State:
https://www.alexanderpen.co.uk/about-the-alexander-technique/the-balanced-resting-state/

The Meditation Trust (UK):
https://www.meditationtrust.com

Books

Benson, Herbert. *The Relaxation Response.* New York: HarperCollins, 2000.

Brach, Tara. *Radical Compassion: Learning to Love Yourself and Your World with the Practice of R.A.I.N.* London: Penguin Random House, 2019.

Burrows, Jonathan. *A Choreographer's Handbook.* London and New York: Routledge, 2010.

Clear, James. *Atomic Habits: An Easy & Proven Way to Build Good Habits & Break Bad Ones.* London: Penguin Random House, 2018.

Cornett, Vanessa. *The Mindful Musician: Mental Skills for Peak Performance.* New York: Oxford University Press, 2019.

Dürckheim, Karlfried Graf. *Hara: The Vital Centre of Man.* Rochester, Vermont: Inner Traditions, 2004.

Farhi, Donna. *The Breathing Book: Good Health and Vitality Through Essential Breath Work.* New York: Owl Books, 1996.

Faulkner, Gordon. *Managing Stress with Qigong.* London: Singing Dragon, 2011.

Fehmi, Les and Jim Robbins. *The Open-Focus Brain: Harnessing the Power of Attention to Heal Mind and Body.* Boulder: Trumpeter, 2008.

Givens, Jerry. *Essential Pranayama: Breathing Techniques for Balance, Healing, and Peace.* Emeryville, California: Rockridge Press, 2020.

Hartley, Aimee. *Breathe Well: Easy and Effective Exercises to Boost Energy, Feel Calmer, More Focused and Productive.* London: Kyle Books, 2020.

Herrigel, Eugen. *Zen in the Art of Archery.* London: Penguin Books, 1985.

Kabat-Zinn, Jon. *Full Catastrophe Living: How to Cope with Stress, Pain and Illness Using Mindfulness Meditation.* London: Piatkus, 2013.

Kaminoff, Leslie and Amy Matthews. *Yoga Anatomy.* Champaign, IL: Human Kinetics, 2012.

Kleinman, Judith and Peter Buckoke. *The Alexander Technique for Musicians.* London, New Delhi, New York, Sydney: Bloomsbury, 2015.

Lam, Kam Chuen. *The Qigong Workbook for Anxiety.* Oakland: New Harbringer Publications, Inc., 2014.

Lely, John and James Saunders. *Word Events: Perspectives on Verbal Notation.* London, New Delhi, New York, Sydney: Bloomsbury, 2012.

Mark, Thomas. *What Every Pianist Needs to Know About the Body.* Chicago: GIA Publications, Inc., 2003.

McKeown, Patrick. *The Breathing Cure: Exercises to Develop New Breathing Habits for a Healthier, Happier and Longer Life.* Galway: OxyAt Books, 2021.

Nachmanovitch, Stephen. *Free Play: Improvisation in Life and Art.* New York: Penguin Putnam Inc., 1990.

Nyman, Michael. *Experimental Music: Cage and Beyond.* New York: Schirmer Books, 1974.

O'Connor, Penny. *Alexander Technique for Actors: A Practical Guide.* London: Nick Hern Books, 2021.

Peters, Steve. *The Chimp Paradox: the Mind Management Programme for Confidence, Success and Happiness.* London: Vermilion, 2012.

Powers, Sarah. *Insight Yoga.* Boulder: Shamhala, 2008.

Rothenberg, Robin. *Restoring Prana: A Therapeutic Guide to Pranayama and Healing Through the Breath for Yoga Therapists, Yoga Teachers and Healthcare Practitioners.* London and Philadelphia: Singing Dragon, 2020.

Schwartz, Richard C. and Martha Sweezy. *Internal Family Systems Therapy: Second Edition.* New York, London: The Guilford Press, 2020.

Steelsmith, Laurie. *Natural Choices for Women's Health: How the Secrets of Natural and Chinese Medicine Can Create a Lifetime of Wellness.* New York: Three Rivers Press, 2005.

Thorburn, Gordon. *Men and Sheds.* London, Cape Town, Frenchs Forest, Auckland: New Holland Publishers, 2003.

Van der Kolk, Bessel. *The Body Keeps the Score: Mind, Brain and Body in the Transformation of Trauma.* London: Penguin, 2015.

Williams, Mark and Danny Penman. *Mindfulness: a Practical Guide to Finding Peace in a Frantic World.* London: Piatkus, 2011.

Acknowledgments

Thank you to my husband Ed Bennett, my yoga
mentors Franziska Boehm, Jerry Givens, Eleonora
Ramsby Herrera, Karina Ayn Mirsky and Sarah
Powers, qigong teachers Jeff Cushing (may you rest in
peace) and Aidan Spencer, Alexander Technique
teachers Pippa Bondy and Penny O'Connor and all the
members of my wellbeing support network. Huge
thank you to Alexandra Franzen, Lindsey Smith and
the whole Tiny Book team for sparking and
supporting this idea, my colleagues, friends and
clients who read drafts, initiated conversations and
challenged me as well as all of my incredible music
mentors, past and present.

I am also grateful to you: students, clients, readers;
past, present and future. Thank you for asking
questions, providing feedback, inspiring me to share
and reading this book.

About the Author

Dr Xenia Pestova Bennett is an internationally active concert pianist and Associate Professor at the University of Nottingham. Described as "a powerhouse of contemporary keyboard repertoire" (*Tempo*), "stunning" (*Wales Arts Review*), "ravishing" (*Pizzicato*) and "remarkably sensuous" (*New Zealand Herald*) in the international press, she has earned a reputation as a leading interpreter of uncompromising repertoire alongside masterpieces from the past. Xenia combines her research and first-hand experience in performance anxiety management with extensive training as a yoga, breathwork and meditation instructor. In addition to performing and teaching, Xenia regularly offers workshops on tools to "befriend" performance and generalised anxiety for individuals, businesses and organisations including the British Association for Performing Arts Medicine; the Contemporary Music Centre (Ireland); Facebook London; Triyoga UK; and higher education institutions around the world including leading music conservatoires. https://xeniapestovabennett.com

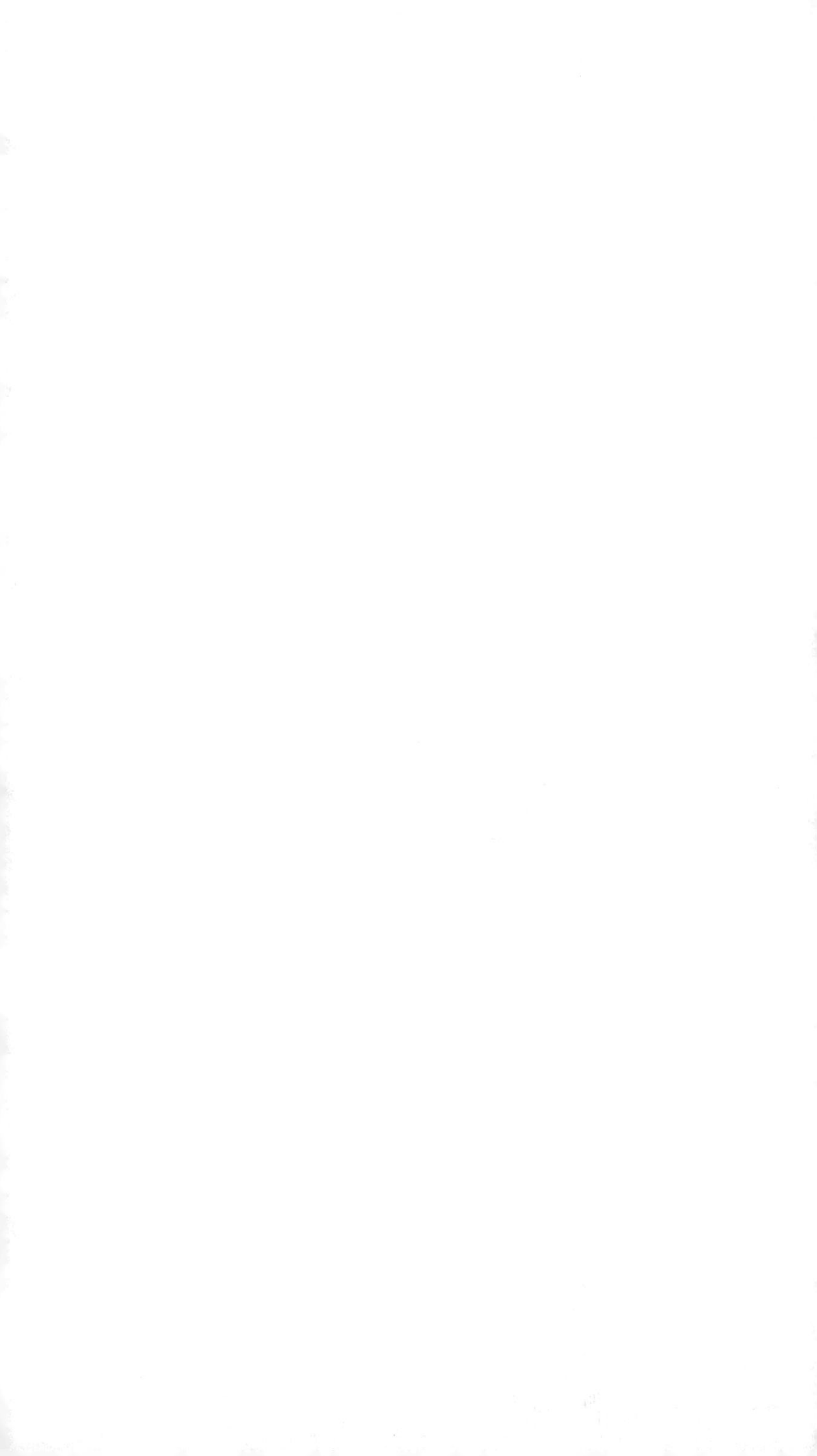